DOG WALK

Modern Curriculum Press
BEGINNING
TO
READ
Series

DOG WALK

Miriam Anne Bourne

Illustrated by Vernon McKissack

MODERN CURRICULUM PRESS

ISBN: 0-8136-5613-3
Printed in the United States of America

5 6 7 8 9 10 11 12   06 05 04 03 02

1-800-321-3106
www.pearsonlearning.com

Nobody at Chippy's house would take him for a walk. So Chippy went to Willie's house and asked him to go for a walk.

Willie was happy to walk with Chippy into the woods. The two dogs held their tails high and their noses close to the ground.

Chippy was old. He walked slowly. His back legs were stiff, and they hurt a little. But he still had a good nose. His old smeller was still good!

Chippy stopped to smell a pile of dry leaves. He pawed the leaves apart. As he pawed, he forgot the hurt in his old back legs.

He dug in the pile faster and faster, and leaves flew in every direction. Chippy sniffed as he dug. It smelled good inside the pile, and it tasted even better.

Then Chippy stopped digging. He lifted
his head. What was Willie doing?
Willie had smelled a rabbit. He was
chasing the rabbit smell this way and
that. Willie's long ears flopped as he
ran. His short legs carried him uphill
and downhill. They carried him under
bushes and over branches.

Chippy watched Willie run. Chippy remembered when he was young. He could chase rabbits then. He could run faster than Willie.

Chippy bit a stick. Never mind. He still had good teeth. His old chewers were still good. He could chew that old stick to pieces!

Deep in the woods Willie yelped. Chippy stopped chewing. Had Willie caught the rabbit?

Chippy trotted along to find Willie. When he came to the stream, he stopped at the bridge. Chippy remembered this stream.

Last spring he had fallen off the bridge into the cold water. He had been stiff for a long time after that.

Now the stream was low. It had not rained for weeks. Chippy was hot. He walked into the stream and lapped some water.

Willie yelped again. Chippy shook himself. He leaped up onto the bank and fell down. His old legs would not leap that high any more.

Chippy remembered when he was young. He could leap onto that bank then. He could leap over fallen logs and stone walls and fences. No fence in the world could keep Chippy in!

Chippy picked himself up and walked toward Willie.

Willie had not caught the rabbit. Instead, Willie was wagging his tail and yelping at a squirrel in a tree. The squirrel dropped a nut on Willie's head. Silly Willie!

Suddenly Chippy saw something move behind a bush. He stood very still. He got ready to pounce.

It was a cat! The cat walked around the bush with a dead mouse in her mouth. Chippy growled his fiercest growl.

The cat stopped and looked at Chippy. Her yellow fur stood on end, but she did not run away. She just crawled slowly under another bush.

Chippy's ears and tail dropped. Did that cat think he was too old to chase her?

Chippy remembered when he was young. He chased cats then. He chased rabbits faster than Willie could chase them. He chased squirrels, too. No squirrel dared drop a nut on Chippy's head.

Suddenly Chippy smelled a strange smell, so he lifted his nose in the air. He heard a strange sound, so his ears went up. He saw a strange sight. Did Willie see it, too?

No. Willie was too busy with the squirrel.

What Chippy saw was a pile of dry leaves.
The pile was making a crackling sound!
Smoke was rising from the leaves. Hot
flames were jumping up.

Chippy backed away from the burning leaves.
He barked once. Then he barked again and
again. Chippy barked loud, quick barks.
His old barker was still good!

Willie stopped yelping and looked at
Chippy. When he saw the flames, he
barked, too.

A door slammed at Chippy's house. Chippy
knew his family was angry at the noise.
But he could not stop himself from barking.

When Chippy's owner saw the flames, he was no longer angry with Chippy. He ran back to the house.

Soon a fire truck raced down the road. Its siren howled. The noise made Chippy and Willie feel like howling. They howled and howled. Nobody told them to keep still.

The fire truck stopped at the edge of the woods. Fire fighters pulled a hose to the fire. A stream of water rushed out of the hose, and the water fell on the burning leaves.

Chippy's family and Willie's family and all the neighbors came to watch.

Chippy and Willie barked and barked until the fire was out.

When the fire fighters left, Chippy was
tired. Barking was hard work for an old
dog. He lay down on the wet leaves. He
rolled over and over in the cool, muddy
earth. It felt good on his hot back.
The mud felt good to Willie, too.

Then Chippy went home to sleep. But
Willie was not tired. He ran off to chase
another rabbit.

That night Chippy lay by the door and looked out at the full moon. The woods were as bright as day. Chippy's family petted and hugged him. They called him a hero. They called him a brave old dog. But nobody would take him for a walk.

So Chippy went to Willie's house. Willie was happy to walk with Chippy into the woods. The two dogs held their tails high and their noses close to the ground.

Miriam Anne Bourne is a former teacher of young children and the author of more than a dozen children's books.

In addition to giving practice with words that most children will recognize, *Dog Walk* uses the 70 enrichment words listed below.

air	digging	hose	rushed
angry	direction	howl(ed, ing)	
apart	downhill	hugged	siren
	dug		slammed
bank		lapped	smeller
barker	earth	leap(ed)	smoke
branches	edge	lifted	sniffed
bridge		logs	stiff
burning	fallen	loud	stone
bush(es)	felt		stream
	fiercest	muddy	suddenly
chase(d, ing)	fighters		
chew(ing)	flames	noise	tasted
chewers	flew	nut	tired
close	flopped		trotted
cool	fur	owner	
crackling			uphill
crawled	ground	pawed	
	growl(ed)	pounce	wagging
dared			world
dead	heard	rising	
deep	hero	rolled	yelp(ed, ing)